Praise for *Pops*

"Dazzling. . . . The novelist's equanimity is so unassailable, and his parenting style so judicious and measured, that lesser men may feel inadequate, hopelessly stuck in the swampy, irrational chafe and fray of day-to-day family life." —*Washington Post*

"Deeply affecting. . . . Chabon is a gifted essayist whose narratives lead to unexpected and resonant conclusions. His work here packs an outsize emotional punch that will stick with readers significantly longer than it takes them to read this slim volume."

—*Publishers Weekly* (starred review)

"Emotionally provocative. . . . [A] literary ode to parenting."

—*Library Journal* (starred review)

"Chabon's book feels like a late-night talk with a friend about how we love our kids and how hopeful we are that we're better dads than we fear."

—Judd Apatow, *New York Times Book Review*

"Thoughtful and moving."

—Mary Carole McCauley, *Baltimore Sun*

"Poignant, often hysterical essays on what it means to be a dad, a son, and a man."

—*People*

"Chabon expertly weaves together past and present events, infusing them with humor, pop culture, and profound observations."

—*Booklist* (starred review)

"Winning, poignant.... Each of its eight essays constructs a telling world, as Chabon trains his keen eye on small family moments that open onto larger issues." —*Boston Globe*

"Combines perfect pitch of tone with an acute eye for detail." —*Kirkus Reviews*

Also by **MICHAEL CHABON**

MICHAEL CHABON

POPS

Fatherhood in Pieces

HARPER ● PERENNIAL

NEW YORK ● LONDON ● TORONTO ● SYDNEY ● NEW DELHI ● AUCKLAND

HARPER PERENNIAL

FIRST HARPER PERENNIAL EDITION PUBLISHED 2019.

Designed by Leah Carlson-Stanisic

Library of Congress Cataloging-in-Publication Data has been applied for.

ISBN 978-0-06-285112-3 (pbk.)

19 20 21 22 23   LSC   10 9 8 7 6 5 4 3 2 1

To my father, and to my children

I've been there and back
And I know how far it is

—RONNIE LANE

CONTENTS

INTRODUCTION: THE OPPOSITE OF WRITING

At a literary party the summer before my first novel was published, I found myself alone with a writer I admired, on the deck of our hosts' house along the Truckee River. People came and went with blue Mexican wineglasses and bottles of beer, but I sensed that, for whatever reason, I had the man's attention.

"I'm going to give you some advice," he told me, a warning edge in his voice.

I said I would appreciate that. I was curious to hear what he had to say, not because I felt in need of advice but as a clue to the mystery of the great man himself. He presented a smooth surface without chinks or toeholds, the studied amiability of someone unaccustomed to giving himself away. Advice might be the only clue I was going to get.

The great man said that his advice was going to be painful—or maybe that was just in his tone—but he knew what he was talking about, and if I wanted to make a go of it as a novelist, I would do well to pay attention. The guy was nearly twice my age, but he was not old. He was young enough, for example, to wear black Chuck Taylors. He was young enough to smile ironically at himself, laying the Polonius routine on some raw hurler of metaphors out of UC Irvine.

"Don't have children," he said. "That's it. Do not." The smile faded, but its ghost lingered a moment in his blue eyes. "That is the whole of the law."

I was due to marry my future ex-wife in under a month; my book would come out the following spring. It turned out that this conjunction of circumstances, in the view of the famous writer, was cause for alarm. Now, marriage was fine—in fact, all of the guy's books were dedicated to his long-suffering wife—but if you were not careful, you would run a serious risk of damaging your career. After this one, he patiently explained, there would be a second novel to write, and second novels were notoriously thornier and more unwieldy than debuts. Following the inevitable sophomore cock-up, if I were lucky and stubborn in the proper measure, I would go on to tackle the magisterial third and fourth novels, and then the quirky fifth, the slim and elegant sixth, the seventh that, in some way, would recapitulate and ring the changes on all its predecessors, and so on, for as long as my stubbornness and luck held out. Unless, of course, I made the fatal mistake of so many would-be young hotshots before me.

"You can write great books," the great man continued. "Or you can have kids. It's up to you."

I nodded, reeling a little at the prophecy he had just laid down for me, a career of struggle and triumph stacked up to the heavens like Babel, book by torturous book.

"I never thought about it that way," I confessed. My future ex-wife and I had gotten as far as the usual drawing up of rotisserie-league baby-name rosters, but no further. Did I need to put an immediate halt to these playful conversations, along with any more earnest ones that might arise? She was a poet, with ambitions of her own.

"Poe," he said. "O'Connor. Welty. None of them had children." This was a list that, by implication, included him; he was a Southerner himself, and he and his beloved dedicatee were childless, too. "Chekhov. Beckett. Woolf."

I tried to muster some counterexamples, but alas, the one who came immediately to mind was my current idol, John Cheever, packed into a house in Ossining with his aggrieved wife and three children. I had just been reading the memoirs of his daughter, Susan. Her childhood had been quietly calamitous, her father's career a farrago of alcoholism, shame, and secret homosexuality. The short stories had over time come unbuttoned, the novels proceeding with the sham dignity and slow gait of drunks trying to pass for sober, while the children alternated between hoping desperately to be seen and trying to keep out of the way. It was at least arguable, I guessed, that the man ought never to have had children at all. I wondered how Susan Cheever would feel about that proposition.

"Put it this way, Michael," the great man said, and then he sketched out the brutal logic: Writing was a practice. The more you wrote, the better a writer you became, and the more books you produced. Excellence plus productivity, that was the formula for sustained success, and time was the coefficient of both. Children, the great man said, were notorious thieves of time. Then there was the question of subject matter, settings, experiences; books were hungry things, and if you stayed too long in any one place, they would consume everything and everyone around you. You needed to keep moving, always onward, a literary Masai driving your ravenous herd of novels. Travel, therefore, was a must, and I should take his word for it, because he had made a careful study: Traveling with children was the world's biggest pain in the ass. Anyway, writers were restless folk. They could not thrive without being able to pick up and go, wherever and whenever it suited them. Writers needed to be irresponsible, ultimately, to everything but the writing, free of commitments to everything but the daily word count. Children, by contrast, needed stability, consistency, routine, and above all, commitment. In short, he was saying, children are the opposite of writing.

"Thomas Mann?" I tried. I had been racking my brain to think of a great writer who was a family man but not calamitously so, like Cheever. My enthusiasm for Mann had faded of late, but I would never forget the rapture of the summer I had spent, five years earlier, climbing *The Magic Mountain*.

"Thomas Mann?" the great man said. He grinned; I had walked right into his trap. "Thomas Mann used to lock himself in his room! Every day! For hours! His children were forbidden to disturb him, on pain of death, and that's barely an exaggeration. His children were a disturbance to him. When he was working, they were a source of pain. I mean, forget the question of getting your work done, is that the kind of *father* you want to be?"

That was an easy one to answer. I knew, without ever having discussed it with my future ex-wife or anyone, the kind of father I wanted to be. Unlike my own father, I would be around for my children whenever they needed me, over breakfast, doing

8

homework, when they learned to swim, to cook, to ride a bicycle; when they cried into their pillows. I would be present in my children's lives. In short, my door would always be open to them. Until now it had never occurred to me that this ambition might be incompatible with the practice of writing.

"Richard Yates," said the great man, preparing to deliver the *tercio de muerte*, like one of Hemingway's matadors. "You know what Richard Yates said?"

Oh, no, I thought. I revered the bleak and gimlet-eyed Yates, for *Easter Parade* and *Revolutionary Road* and *Eleven Kinds of Loneliness*; no way was this going to be anything but grim.

"'You lose a book,'" the great man quoted, or paraphrased, or possibly invented himself, "'for every child.'"

Now the great man smiled. He could see the effect that his words were having on me as I stood there trying to reckon how many books I stood, or would stand, to lose. My future ex-wife and I had settled on two names, one male, one female. This suggested a worst case of two books, two books erased, wiped away by the universal solvent of children. I supposed I could live with that. But what if, after the first two, there was an "accident," too much wine in the afternoon, a failure of birth control; and what if, God forbid, that third pregnancy turned out to be twins? Suddenly, in my imagination, I was clinging to the base of that half-built Babel, up to my ankles in a roiling surf of babies and brats, the non-author of an entire shelf of great novels I would never be able to write, any one of them conceivably my masterpiece.

"All right, Michael, you think about it," said the great man in that accent like butter on a warm biscuit. His work was done. He patted me on the shoulder, rattled the last half-inch of Dos Equis in his bottle, and went back inside the house, confident of having saved—or at least of having frightened—another lost lamb.

I have a vague recollection of reporting this conversation afterward to my future ex-wife, and of our laughing it off as arrogant self-justification or, perhaps, more pitiably, making virtue of necessity. We got married, moved a few times, got divorced. I managed to snatch a handful of gently *farbisn* short stories out of that Gilliganesque pleasure cruise, though the second novel I attempted to build and launch over the course of those years, a would-be epic, sank like a vast unseaworthy dreadnought, unsalvageable, to the bottom of my soul. Fortunately, there were no children to blame for that shipwreck. A couple of years later I married again, and over the quarter century that has followed, while fathering four children, I've managed to turn out fourteen books.

Should there be eighteen?

Is the creative wistfulness that sometimes comes over me after a rough night at the keyboard, that feeling of having somehow wandered by mistake into the wrong book, a kind of mourning for the loss of those other, phantom-limb novels, the ones that my children stole? It's certainly the case that if one were to plot on a graph my declining output of short stories over the past two decades alongside my rising output of children, the resulting X would seem to mark the scene of a crime. But the reason I almost never write short stories anymore isn't that my children are time thieves. It's that my children are expensive, and short stories just don't pay very well. I can't afford to write short stories anymore.

And those four "lost" novels predicted by the great man's theory all those years ago? (Setting aside for the moment the question of whether you can lose something you never had, and the fact that going around telling people "You lose a book for every child" sounds like exactly the kind of romantically unromantic self-pity you would expect from the full-blown raging alcoholic that Richard Yates had apparently become by the end of his life.)

If I had followed the great man's advice and never burdened myself with the gift of my children, or if I had never written any novels at all, in the long run the result would have been the same as the result will be for me here, having made the choice I made: I will die; and the world in its violence and serenity will roll on, through the endless indifference of space; and it will take only one hundred of its circuits around the sun to turn the six of us, who loved each other, to dust, and consign to oblivion all but a scant few of the thousands upon thousands of novels and short stories written and published during our lifetimes. If none of my books turns out to be among that bright remnant because I allowed my children to steal my time, narrow my compass, and curtail my freedom, I'm all right with that. Once they're written, my books, unlike my children, hold no wonder for me; no mystery resides in them. Unlike my children, my books are cruelly unforgiving of my weaknesses, failings, and flaws of character. Most of all, my books, unlike my children, do not love me back. Anyway, if, one hundred years hence, those books lie moldering and forgotten, I'll never know. That's the problem, in the end, with putting all your chips on posterity: You never stick around long enough to enjoy it.

LITTLE MAN

Half an hour late, and just ahead of his minder—he was always a step ahead of his ponderous old minder—Abraham Chabon sauntered into the room where the designer Virgil Abloh was giving a private preview of Off-White's collection for spring/summer 2017 to a small group of reporters, editorial directors, and fashion buyers. Abe's manner was self-conscious, his cheeks flushed, but if his movements were a bit constrained, they had an undeniable grace. "Saunter" was really the only word for it.

"Now, this dude here, that's what I'm talking about," Abloh said, smiling at Abe from the center of the room, the attic of an old photo studio in the Latin Quarter: crisscrossing steel beams, wide pine floorboards, every surface radiant with whitewash except for the gridded slant of windows in the steep-pitched roof. From their folding chairs opposite the atelier windows, the buyers and editors turned to see what Abloh was talking about. So did the four male models lined up and slouching artfully in front of the people in the folding chairs. By the time his minder caught up with him, everyone in the room seemed to have their eyes on Abe. Prompt people never get to make grand entrances.

"Come over here," Abloh said. Abloh was a big man, solidly built, an architect by training who had emerged in the early 2000s from the fizzy intellectual nimbus—one third hip-hop, one third hustle, one third McLarenesque inside joke—surrounding fellow Chicagoan Kanye West. Abloh had made a name for himself in fashion along the avant-garde perimeter of streetwear, screen-printing diagonal crosswalk stripes and cryptic mottoes onto blank Champion tees and dead-stock Rugby Ralph Lauren flannel shirts that he resold for dizzying multiples of their original retail price. Abe thought Virgil Abloh was "lit," the highest accolade he could award to anyone or anything. "Come right on over here. Hey, look at you!"

Abe went on over, sleeves rolled, hands thrust into his pockets, tails of his pale gray-green shirt freshly tucked into the waist of his gray twill trousers. In front, the shirt lay flat and trim, but it was a little too big, and at the back, it bellied out over the top of his skinny black belt. It was Maison Margiela, cleanly tailored, with a narrow collar and covered buttons that gave it a minimalist sleekness. Abe had bought it the day before, on sale, at a shop in Le Marais called Tom Greyhound. He wore a pair of $400 silver Adidas by Raf Simons purchased for $250 on adidasx.com and a pair of Off-White athletic socks. He had pulled the socks up to his knees, where they met the rolled-up cuffs of his trouser legs, vintage-newsboy-style. Abe had earned the money to pay for the "Rafs" by raking leaves for neighbors, organizing drawers and closets around the house, running errands, and other odd jobs. His parents had given him, on the occasion of his bar mitzvah, the cash he'd used to buy the Margiela shirt, and the trousers had actually been repurposed from his Appaman bar mitzvah suit. Abe was thirteen years and three months old, and he did not need to be told, by Virgil Abloh or anyone else, to look at himself. He knew exactly how he looked.

"Hi," Abe said to Abloh in his husky voice—low-pitched and raspy all his life, heading even lower now and given, at the moment, to random breaking—"I'm Abe."

Some of the people in the room already knew Abe—which tended to get pronounced Ah-*bay*, like the surname of the Japanese prime minister, by the French staffers who put his name on the guest lists for the fourteen shows he attended over the course of Paris Men's Fashion Week. They had met him or seen him around. He was almost always, and by far, the youngest person in the audience, and likely would have stood out for that reason alone, even if he had not dressed himself with such evident consideration and casual art. But it was his clothes and the way he wore them that elicited reporters' attention, and a few had taken enough of an interest to ask him some questions, on the record. The questions tended to run along the same lines: What had he thought of this or that particular collection? What got him interested in clothes? Did he hope to be a fashion designer one day? Why had he come to Fashion Week?

I'm here with my dad, it's my bar mitzvah present, he's a writer, and he's writing about our trip to Fashion Week for GQ. I know I want to do something in fashion, but I don't know what, maybe design; I do make sketches, mostly streetwear, I like to use fabrics and patterns you kind of wouldn't expect, like, I don't know, a Japanese textile pattern for a bomber jacket, or glen-plaid overalls. My older brother got me interested in clothes, it started with sneakers and then it kind of grew, and now I know more about men's fashion than he does. I thought the collection was interesting or I thought it was awesome or I thought it was a little boring, you know, it didn't really stand out, we've seen a lot of trench coats already this week or The quality of the tailoring didn't seem very good or I thought it was insane or It was fire or It was totally lit.

Abe's minder noticed that, when talking to

reporters, Abe almost always found a way to mention the leaf-raking and drawer-organizing, conscious of the atmosphere of privilege and extravagance that permeated the world of fashion. He knew that for a lot of kids his age—good friends of his among them—the price of a pair of "fire" sneakers represented a greater and more important sacrifice than it would for him and his family. But he never directly addressed the ethics of his wearing a shirt that had cost him $225 on sale. He did not offer profound insights into the economics or meaning of style like some pocket-size Roland Barthes bursting with critique and paradox.

Abe was just a kid who loved clothes. He loved talking about them, looking at them, and wearing them, and when it came to men's clothing, in particular the hipper precincts of streetwear, he knew his shit. He could trace the career path of Raf Simons, from Raf to Jil Sander to Dior and now to Calvin Klein. He could identify on sight the designers of countless individual articles of men's clothing—sneakers, shirts, jackets, pants—and when he didn't know for sure, the guesses he made were informed, reasoned, and often correct.

He seemed to have memorized a dense tidal chart of recent fashion trends as they ebbed and flooded, witheringly dismissing a runway offering as "fine, for 2014" or "already kind of played out last year." His taste as reflected in the clothes he wore was impeccable, interesting, and, in its way, fearless.

It takes a profound love of clothes, and some fairly decent luck, to stumble on somebody who wants to converse about cutting-edge men's fashion at a Rush concert, and yet a year before his trip to Paris, in the aftermath of the Canadian band's last show at Madison Square Garden, Abe had managed to stumble on John Varvatos. Abe had spent that day leading his bemused minder on a pilgrimage through SoHo, from Supreme to Bape to Saint Laurent to Y-3, and now, ears still ringing from the final encore ("Working Man"), Abe reported in detail to Varvatos, with annotations and commentary, on all the looks he had seen downtown. When he was through, Varvatos had turned to Abe's minder—a major Rush fan who was, of course, also Abe's father—and said, "Where'd you *get* this kid?"

"I really have no idea," I said.

Abe had shown up late to his family, too, the fourth of four, graced with a sister on either side of the elder brother. By the time a fourth child comes along, the siblings have usually managed among them to stake out a wide swath of traits, talents, crotchets, flaws, phobias, and strengths. Finding one's difference can often be a fourth child's particular burden and challenge.

For Abe it never seemed to be a challenge at all, and if it was a burden, it was also a gift: From the moment he became himself, what made Abe different—from his siblings, from classmates, from most of the children who have ever lived—was the degree of comfort he felt with being different. Everybody wants to stand out from the crowd, but so few of us have the knack, and fewer still the stomach for bearing up under the crush of conformity. It was always Abe's rare gift not just to stand out and bear up but to do those things with panache. And the way in which he expressed his difference most reliably, and with the greatest panache, was through dressing up.

When he was very little—as for so many little boys—"dressing up" meant "superhero." At three he was firmly of the opinion that a bright-yellow-and-sky-blue Wolverine costume, or a lop-eared bat cowl, was appropriate attire for any occasion. Later there was an intense dalliance with a splendid old-school singing-cowboy-type western getup—black hat, red shirt embroidered in white, black vest and chaps with chrome conchos, black boots. When he started kindergarten, however, he found that the wearing of costumes to school was not merely discouraged, or permitted only on special days, as in preschool: It was forbidden. It would also, undoubtedly, have incurred an intolerable amount of mockery. Abe's response was to devise, instinctively and privately, what amounted to a kind of secret costume that would fall just within the bounds of "ordinary attire" and school policy. Over the next few years, with increasing frequency, he went to school dressed up as a man—a stylish man.

He had only vague, somewhat cartoonish notions about what constituted adult-male style, centered around certain key articles of clothing, chief among them fedoras, cardigans, button-front shirts, suspenders, and bow ties. He had a little tweed blazer that was a source of deep power for him, as deep as the power of the armor to Marvel's Iron Man. It had a crest embroidered on a patch over the breast pocket, and it made him very happy. By third grade, he was wearing his man costume to school almost every day. There was teasing; one of his two little snap-brims got snatched off his head now and then and tossed around the playground. But the teasing never exceeded Abe's ability or willingness to withstand it, or the joy that he derived from losing himself in clothes. And his stubborn persistence established a pattern that was thereafter repeated as his taste grew more refined and sophisticated: Little by little, one by one among the other boys in his class, fedoras would crop up, a porkpie here, a trilby there. It was not unusual to spot one of Abe's former tormentors sporting a cardigan or a clip-on tie.

Some nights I used to stand in the doorway of his bedroom, watching him thoughtfully edit the outfit he planned to wear to school the next day. He would lay out its components, making a kind of flat self-portrait on the bedroom floor—oxford shirt tucked inside of cotton sport coat, extra-slim pants (with the adjustable elastic straps inside the waistband stretched to button at the very last hole), argyle socks, the whole thing topped by the ubiquitous hat—and I would try to understand what the kid got out of dressing up every day like a pint-size Ronald Colman out for a tramp across the countryside of Ruritania. Did he like the attention, even if it was negative? Was he trying, by means of the clothes, to differentiate himself from the other boys, or were the clothes merely the readiest expression, to him, of his having been *born* different? Was he trying to set himself apart, or could he simply not help it?

Around the time when Abe was making the transition to middle school, my elder son began to take a strong interest in clothes, particularly streetwear, fed by a burgeoning interest (shared by Abe) in hip-hop. A kind of golden age of streetwear was under way, exemplified by brands such as Supreme, Palace, and A Bathing Ape, manifested through "collabs" between major sneaker manufacturers and the edgier, top-tier designers like Rick Owens and Raf Simons, and represented by hip-hop tastemakers like A$AP Rocky and the now disgraced Ian Connor. Abe's elder brother opened the door to this world—Virgil Abloh's world—and Abe sauntered right in.

Even as he followed his brother into this trend-driven, icon-imitating world, Abe worked to maintain his standard of idiosyncrasy, of standing out, freely incorporating floral patterns, vintage scarves, and the color pink into the outfits he wore into the heteronormative jaws of seventh grade. Small for his age—barely a men's size XS—Abe often had trouble finding anything "fire," in the way of menswear, that would fit him. So he would shop the women's racks, with a sharply editorial eye; a women's XS, he could make work. The

Maison Margiela shirt he wore at the Off-White preview was women's wear, and he had chanced upon another favorite shirt, a Tigran Avetisyan, while browsing one of the women's-clothing rooms at Opening Ceremony in L.A.

The sight of him, hanging around the neighborhood with a friend, looking so at ease in the flowing cream-black-and-gray Avetisyan shirt with its bold bands of red at the collar and cuffs and wild graphic pattern, made me realize that I almost never saw boys his age wearing anything remotely like it, wearing anything but a T-shirt or an athletic jersey, a hoodie or a flannel. The mantle of uniformity lay vast and heavy across the shoulders of adolescent boys (how vast, how heavy, I remembered well). As before—even worse than before—Abe suffered taunts and teasing for his style of dress and his love of style. But he did not back down; he doubled down. He flew the freak flag of his Tigran Avetisyan shirt high. And though I couldn't fathom the impulse driving my kid to expose himself every day to mockery and verbal abuse at school, I admired him for not surrendering, and in time

I came to understand the nature of my job as the father of this sartorial wild child: I didn't *need* to fathom Abe or his stylistic impulses; I needed only to let him go where they took him and, for as long as he needed me, to follow along behind.

There was only one flaw, as far as Abe was concerned, in the week he spent going to fashion shows: His poky old minder, making him late. His minder was not having anywhere near as great a time. His minder was hot and bored. Most of all, his minder did not, fundamentally, really give all that much of a fuck about fashion. Clothes, sure. His minder found pleasure in thrift-shopping for vintage western shirts or Hermès neckties, in wearing his favorite Shipley & Halmos suits (gray cashmere, tan corduroy), his Paul Smith shirts and shoulder bag. Less pleasure, perhaps, than he found in books, or records, or cooking, or watching old movies with his wife, but pleasure nonetheless. Clothes were all right with Abe's minder. But they were nothing to build a religion, a hobby, or even a decent obsession around.

Then, one warm June week in Paris, Abe's minder attended his first Men's Fashion Week and discovered that he understood even less. Fashion shows had an unexpected sideshow-freaks-on-parade quality, and when they were not pompous or eccentric, they were just plain goofy. You drove all the way across Paris to get to the venue—a special mapping algorithm seemed to have been employed to ensure that every show was held as far as possible from its predecessor and its successor on the schedule—through the heat of a Paris summer, arrived late yet still waited around outside until your feet hurt, guaranteeing you would be late for the next show, too. Then you sat in a dark, loud, hot, crowded room for another twenty minutes. The lights came on and the music pounded. There would be a wall made out of old car headlights and a sonic wall of EDM, and a bunch of tall, bony, pouting young men with a studied air of opiate addiction would come striding past you, swinging their arms like little boys pretending to walk like their dads in a game of playing house. This gait was meant to read as "fierce," someone explained to Abe's minder, as was the expression on the models' faces, a universal stony blank, tinged with rouge, onto which it was forbidden to affix a smile.

The looks they modeled ranged in effect from preposterous to functional to arresting, often in the same show. Sometimes the music would be not EDM but Neil Young or Leonard Cohen or the amazing Japanese neo-psychedelic band Kikagaku Moyo.

At the Paul Smith show, the models just walked—sauntered, really—like the good-looking young dudes they were, and when they saw somebody they knew in the audience, or when they just felt good in the beautiful suits and shirts Paul Smith had dressed them in, they would—heretically—smile. Issey Miyake gave you a first-aid chemical cold pack to break and lay against the sweaty nape of your neck. Once—at the Y-3 show—the pants were inflatable. The whole show would be over in ten minutes, yet it would still run overtime, and then you got back into a taxi and rushed algorithmically across town. It was kind of like Disneyland, but instead of a three-minute log flume or roller coaster, you got inflatable pants.

Toward the end of one long and particularly trying four-show day for Abe's minder, Abe began to hear about yet another show he was keen to attend. It started at eight p.m. and it would be the last of the day. Abe's minder felt strongly that he had already experienced his last show of the day.

"It's Stéphane Ashpool of Pigalle—he's a really interesting new designer," Abe said. "Everyone says his show last year was amazing. Please, Dad?"

But Abe's minder had hardened his heart against Stéphane Ashpool. Fortunately for Abe, certain members of the editorial staff of *GQ* magazine, who had been telling Abe about last year's Pigalle show and generally testing, to their apparent satisfaction, the breadth and depth of his knowledge of men's clothing, offered to let him come along with them to this year's. There was room in the car. They would see to it that he would be returned to his minder at the rendezvous point, a party at the Musée Picasso.

It turned out that Abe's minder possibly made

the wrong decision in choosing not to go to the Pigalle show. A few hours later, Abe showed up at the Picasso vibrating with excitement about the clothes he had seen and, even more, about the remarkable way they had been presented. Instead of the usual solemn palace or dark box pounding with electronica, instead of the usual runway, the Pigalle show had been presented outdoors, at the back of a museum, in a garden. It had taken the form of a faux wedding party, with musicians and a wedding canopy and little round café tables for all the "guests." Food was served. The evening felt cool. Abe had sat with the people from *GQ* and been caught up in the night and the company and the beautiful clothes.

"It was like being at a play," he said. "But also being in it."

"You need to go stand over there," Virgil Abloh told Abe. He pointed at the line of male models, who looked a little taken aback at the turn things had taken but made room for Abe in their ranks.

Abe laughed, and the flush in his cheeks deepened, but he did as he was told, without apparent hesitation or awkwardness. The laughter and the hectic color were not due to embarrassment; Abe was excited and pleased. The presence on his feet of Off-White socks was hardly an accident. Abe was not the kind of boy who would go to a baseball game with his mitt, hoping that a foul ball might come his way and fantasizing that if one did, he would snatch it from the air with such evident skill that he would be offered, on the spot, a contract to play for the home team, but there was definitely an aspect in this moment of the dream come true.

And really, he had nothing to be embarrassed about. Sure, these models were nearly twice his height, and very good-looking, but with all due respect to Virgil Abloh and his stylists, none of the models was dressed any better—or looked more comfortable in what he was wearing—than Abe. Over the past two days of attending shows with his minder, Abe had paid close attention to everything that came down the runways, but he had, if anything, made an even more careful study

35

of clothes worn by certain young men one saw waiting around outside the venues, standing in line with their elaborate tickets until the people with the clipboards said it was time to go inside. The models on the runways had without question been *fashionably* dressed—from the shaggy yellow Muppet pants and clown-emblazoned transparent breastplates at the Walter Van Beirendonck show to the hyper-flared trousers and fringed jackets *chez* Dries Van Noten to the Möbius-meets–*Logan's Run* 1970s post-apocalypse gear on view at the Rick Owens show, his models swaggering gloomily through the subterranean venue like young volunteers to be fed to the robot god, wearing sneakers so enormous that a couple of them tripped over their own toes—but these guys who caught Abe's eye, always two or three or four of them scattered among the waiting crowds, had *style*. The clothes they wore were their own, chosen and tweaked and assembled by them from their own drawers and closets. Often these looks were built around a single stunning, no doubt exorbitant garment, a dazzling scarlet silk tracksuit, say, paisleyed with light blue and peach paramecia and paired with a yellow bandanna worn as a neckerchief.

The looks Abe made the closest study of were the eclectic ones, the ones that had been assembled out of disparate, perhaps more affordable elements into a surprising whole. One of Abe's favorites had belonged to a handsome black dude he saw outside the Van Beirendonck show. He had a bushy beard and wore an odd felt hat with a broad brim and broad diagonal pleats around its crown, a cross between an Amish number and a Jell-O mold. Over a black mesh undershirt he had on a gold-and-green plaid blazer, down the front of which he had stitched groups of black thread in parallel lines like guitar strings. He had stacked tribal bracelets on his wrists, silver tribal earrings curled in his earlobes, and he wore round gold granny glasses. His moon-boot-style sneakers had been precisely distressed, and his black pin-striped trousers, belted with a length of red-and-white jump rope, he wore rolled to the knee. It was a mad jumble of pieces of this and that from here and there, but somehow it all went together. It expressed an idea, and the idea it expressed was not Rick Owens's idea or Juun.J's idea but all the bits and pieces from here and there that made up the mind and history of the guy who had put them on.

Abe had learned a lot from studying this guy's look and the looks of the other dandies—for that was what they were, unpaid, unsponsored, there only to see and be seen and hoist their colors on the humid afternoon air—who showed up for the shows. Every night he had come home and gone through his suitcase, reviewing the elements of the wardrobe he'd brought with him (with a few fresh additions; it was the week of the *soldes*), combining and recombining them, laying out his little self-portrait on the floor. When he woke up in the morning, he would have changed his mind about something, or a sudden inspiration would strike. The look he had chosen for the Off-White preview had been tested and revised, in his mind and on his body, and it said whatever it was about himself that he had managed, at this early and still inarticulate moment in the history of his soul, to say. It would bear up to scrutiny. It had been designed to bear up to scrutiny. Indeed, it had been designed to *invite* scrutiny, not of the look itself but of the person inside it. His clothes were not *on* the outside of his body; they *were*—for now—the outside of his body. They were the visible form taken by the way he chose to define himself. None of the gawky young models, standing around flat-footed and hunch-shouldered with their assigned coats and jackets and baggy shorts hanging off them like drop cloths thrown over a dining room set, could say that. Even Virgil Abloh, in his black sweats and black T-shirt, seemed to be wearing Off-White.

Virgil Abloh asked Abe where he was from. Abe said that he was from Oakland. That was not quite true; Abe lived in Berkeley, one block from the Oakland-Berkeley line.

Undoubtedly he thought, not without reason, that Oakland sounded, and was, cooler than Berkeley as a place for one to be from. Oakland was the Black Panthers, the impassive cartoon masks thrown up on freeway embankments by graffiti artist GATS, and heroes of hip-hop like Too Short, Mac Dre, Richie Rich, and the Hieroglyphics collective.

Berkeley was bearded dudes wearing drug rugs and drawstring pants in the drum circle at the Ashby BART on Saturday mornings.

"This young man understands the idea, here," Virgil Abloh told the reporters, pens poised over their notepads. "This is what I'm trying to do." Abloh invited his assembled guests to consider Abe's look from the ground up. The models were trying to suppress smiles now and not in all cases succeeding.

"First of all," Abloh said, "you got the Adidas—*hold on!*" He went in for a closer look at Abe's shoes. "You wearing *Rafs*?" He offered Abe a congratulatory fist bump. Abe graciously accepted it. "You got the sneakers, and the athletic socks—the *right* athletic socks." He grinned; Abe beamed. The people in the folding chairs laughed. "So far, everything is coming out of the streetwear context. But then up at the top, the look is something much more tailored. For the young dudes, they're coming out of streetwear labels. Supreme, Bape . . . That's where it starts, right?"

He checked with Abe, who duly and truthfully

nodded. "But now they're thinking, maybe without getting too expensive, maybe they could take it to a higher level. Good," he said to Abe. "Thank you. Go on, now, go have a seat."

Two days and five shows later Abe arrived late for the Off-White show. He had been melancholy all day, and now, as we arrived to find the show halfway over, he sank even further. I felt badly; I had kept us too long at the previous show, Paul Smith.

After the show ended, Abe caught sight of Virgil Abloh backstage, but the designer was surrounded by press and fans. He nodded and smiled at Abe, but they didn't get the chance to speak again. Fashion Week was over. It was time to go home.

"I don't want to go home," Abe said.

"I know," I said. "Paris is fun."

"It's not that."

"It's been so exciting for you," I suggested. "You don't want it to end."

"Yeah. No, it's not that."

"What's wrong?" I said. "Tell me, buddy."

But he didn't want to talk about it. We rode in a

taxi back to our rented apartment in the 12th Ar-
rondissement. Abe slowly packed up his clothes
and laid out the jeans and T-shirt that he planned
to wear on the flight home. He grew more silent
and sank even deeper into whatever was eating
him. He grew tearful. We had an argument. I was
tired of fashion and fashion shows. I could feel
only that I had had enough and that I wanted to
leave and be done. It was hard for me to imagine
feeling any other way.

"We had a good time," I said. "You got to do a lot
of fun things and meet cool people. You got some
nice things to wear. You were in Paris. Now it's
time to go home. Come on."

"I don't want to go back," he said.

"We'll come back to Paris. When you grow up,
you can live here."

"It's not Paris. It's not the clothes."

"What is it?"

"The Pigalle show," he said.

"That was your favorite. I wish I'd gone."

He looked at me, a funny expression on his face.
I realized that the reason he'd had such a great

time that night was because I had *not* been present. I had not been his father or his friend this past week. I had been only his minder. I was a drag to have around a fashion show, and because I could not enter fully into the spirit of the occasion, neither could Abe. He was worrying about me, watching me, wondering whether I was having a good time or not, whether I thought the shaggy Muppet pants, for example, were as stupid as the look on my face seemed to suggest.

"It wasn't the show, really," I suggested as his eyes filled with tears. "Was it? It was the people you were with, the *GQ* guys, the buyers, that dude who owns Wild Style."

"They get it," he said. "They know everything about all the designers, and the house, and that's what they care about. They love to talk about clothes. They love clothes."

You are born into a family and those are your people, and they know you and they love you, and if you are lucky, they even on occasion manage to understand you. And that ought to be enough. But it is never enough. Abe had not been dressing up, styling himself, for all these years because he was trying to prove how different he was from everyone else. He did it in the hope of attracting the attention of somebody else—somewhere, someday—who was the *same*. He was not flying his freak flag; he was sending up a flare, hoping for rescue, for company in the solitude of his passion.

"You were with your people. You found them," I said.

He nodded.

"That's good," I said. "You're early."

ADVENTURES IN
EUPHEMISM

Do you remember the guy in a university town who thought it was a good idea to go through the text of *Huckleberry Finn*, editing it so that each instance of the word "nigger" was replaced with something less offensive? Not the professor at Auburn. Another guy. The one writing this sentence.

Tom Sawyer was bedtime reading for me and my two youngest kids (son and daughter, then seven and nine) a few summers back. Of course we all loved it. It has some slow bits and some prolonged bouts of humor (Tom's lovesickness, his punctilio about make-believe) that must have felt at least a *little* labored even back in 1876, when it often took weeks or months for a punch line to arrive. But it's exciting and funny and often surprisingly tender,

even capital-R Romantic, and the classic bits—
the fence, the Bible-study tickets, the cave, the
murder—appear to have lost none of their power
to delight and scare children who dwell in a world
of childhood so alien from that of Tom and Huck,
half-feral in their liberty, alongside whom my own
children seem like dogs in a run, no longer even
straining at their cable.

Reading *Tom Sawyer* occupied the entire sum-
mer, and during that time I don't remember wres-
tling at all with the question of what to say out
loud, with my actual lips and tongue, when my
eyes arrived at that strange little word. A cursory
search of Google Books suggests that it makes a
total of only eight appearances in the entire book,
which is, after all, not told by a backcountry boy in
his own dialect but narrated, with a great deal of
mock decorum, in the third person. Eight is prob-
ably fairly close to the number of times that I have
said "nigger" in my life, never once without some
kind of ironizing or sterilizing quotation marks
of tone fitted carefully around it. At those fleet-
ing moments when I encountered the word while

reading *Tom Sawyer* to the children, I would sub-stitute, without missing a beat or losing any literal meaning, "slave." It was no big thing. The kids had no idea that a switcheroo had been run on them.

But then we finished *Tom Sawyer,* and they had loved it, most especially the character of Huckle-berry Finn, so much that they begged me to carry on to the eponymous sequel, starting the very next night.

"I don't know," I said. "It's a little bit more of a grown-up book."

It had been at least fifteen years since I'd read it last, and my memories of it were pretty vague. I was kind of repeating the conventional wisdom (which turned out, in my view, to be questionable—apart from the narrative voice, huge stretches of *Huckleberry Finn* don't feel all that different from *Tom Sawyer,* especially toward the end, after Tom and his punctilio make their annoying return. The Duke and Dauphin and the feuding families com-plicate the book in ways that my kids needed help to understand. And then there are a few incredi-bly profound passages, above all the famous one in which Huck wrestles with the situational evil of absolute good as he determines to help Jim get free). But I knew—half-recollected, half-intuited—that there was some thorniness, that something in the book was going to complicate bedtime.

We encountered the first of what must be at least two hundred instances of the bedeviled word on page six, along with Jim himself. *Now* I remembered!

I flipped ahead, finding the word on almost every other page, twice or three times a page. The damned thing was lousy with it.

"Guys," I said, putting the book down. "We need to talk about this."

I explained to them that because this book was written in Huck's own voice, and because, in the time and place of its setting, people of both races commonly referred to black people as "niggers," and because there were a number of black characters, major and minor, in the book, I was going to be obliged to say, or not to say, that word a great many times. I explained that saying the word made me extremely uncomfortable, that it was not a word I

ever used, that some black people still used it some-
times to refer to each other, but that was impor-
tantly different, and that black people I had known
were just as uncomfortable using the word around
white people as white people were using it around
them. I told them about my childhood friend Harry,
who, when discussing the Richard Pryor album
Bicentennial Nigger with me, a fellow Pryor fan but,
unlike Harry, a white boy, used to refer to it by the
safe code name of "Bice."

Next I reminded them that Mark Twain was
a great artist, a moral man, and, furthermore, an
accurate writer. I said that as a writer myself, I
was driven insane by the idea of somebody taking
the words I had worked so hard to get absolutely
correct and spatchcocking in whatever nonsense
made them comfortable. Then I asked my kids
what they thought I ought to do whenever I arrived
at the word over the course of the next few months.
I told them how I had substituted "slave" while we
were reading *Tom Sawyer*, but that in this book,
the word was going to mean so vastly much more,
and less, than that.

"You know what word *I'm* uncomfortable saying?" said my daughter, the nine-year-old. "*Negro.*"

I remembered the earliest days of my consciousness of black people, when that was still, fadingly, a proper term. It had long since acquired distinct overtones of offensiveness, though it was not remotely, I thought, taboo. I could say it without feeling like I was licking a battery.

"Negro," I said. I really did not know what else to do. "All right, let's give that a try."

So we did, and stuck with it, and it kind of worked, but every time I said "Negro," I wondered if they, my new companions in bad faith, were feeling the acid charge of the true word in their minds.

"Hey, Dad," the little guy said at one point. "How come if you can't say you-know-what, when you were reading *Tom Sawyer* you kept saying INJUN Joe, because that's offensive, too."

"Because I'm an ass," I said. Only I didn't say "ass."

I was with my elder daughter, then fifteen, in the Peet's on Telegraph Avenue, with a big Saturday-afternoon crowd, and as we waited for the barista to get to our orders, I started looking around at the other customers with a fresh and appreciative eye for the numerous freakazoids among them.

I had just returned from a trip to a middle-size city deep in the middle of the country, where the people keep their freaky on the inside, deep down where it tends to fester and gasify. Now I felt that I was back among my kind. There was the lady in a coral fake-fur bonnet that featured pink hamster ears. There was the whippet-thin tall guy with the chains and the leather and a haircut like the Sydney Opera House dyed black, knitting something enigmatic—a cock sock, was my guess. At a table in a corner by himself sat a quietly ranting theorist of some subject understood only by him and his invisible interlocutor. And then there were my daughter and me. She was wearing giant flare jeans, a T-shirt that said SPECIAL CARE OR-THOPEDICS on the back, a raspberry pillbox hat with a black net veil and a big pouf of black tulle at the back, and plaid rubber rain boots, even though it wasn't raining. I don't have a really clear picture in my mind of the way I look—no clearer than the view you get of a house when you look out one of its windows—but I travel pretty frequently into the deep middle of the country. And every so often while I'm there, somebody will let slip an observation that seems to suggest I may give some indication of being a Northern California freakazoid, with my long hair, my scruffy beard, my pointy shoes, my pink shirts, my man purse, et cetera.

I felt like telling my daughter that she ought to be grateful she was getting to grow up in Berkeley, where, if you are fourteen and feel like wearing a crazy Jayne Mansfield hat and rubber boots down the street in broad daylight, that is okay with your fellow citizens. Crazy is a choice they can get behind; indeed, they might on balance be inclined to insist on it. So I told her. "You're lucky you get to grow up here. You can be as weird as you want to."

"I should probably be even weirder," she said a little sadly. "It's kind of a waste."

"Just be glad we don't live in Middleburg," I said, referring (though not pseudonymously) to the town from which I had, as I say, recently returned. And I shuddered, only partly for effect. "Man."

"Scary normal?"

"So scary normal."

Now, this characterization was no doubt grossly unfair to the good people of Middleburg. Everybody there had been extremely kind and generous to me. They were, in many instances, literate and enthusiastic people, not to mention hospitable, solicitous, polite, and warm. They were proud of their city and all of its many advantages.

It was not their fault that the whole time I was there, I felt like a kind of animated human scrawl moving across the ruled blue lines of their community. It was not their fault that I entered the atmosphere of their lives and landed on their homely planet as an alien probe, with all my instrumentation—recording devices, analysis units, story samplers—turned up to high gain. And it certainly was not their fault that I have spent my entire life, from the dawn of consciousness until this very moment, even here in hamster-eared Berkeley, feeling totally weird.

When I was ten years old, I read Edgar Allan Poe's verse for the first time and immediately decided (though that verb implies far more consciousness than was actually involved) that I was the poet's living reincarnation. I must have been, for I, I mean he, had written the lines:

> *From Childhood's hour I have not been*
> *As others were—I have not seen*
> *As others saw—I could not bring*
> *My passions from a common spring—*

The hair stood up on my nape as I read those words from "Alone," as did the neck hairs, I'm sure, of ten thousand other kids all around the world at that very moment, in the lonely redoubts of the solitudes we all shared with poor old Edgar Poe (even in Middleburg). Every crowded room I have ever entered, every public space I have ever crossed, every gathering I have ever attended— everywhere I interact with other people, except at the very heart, the absolute Middleburg, of my own family—I have done so with the consciousness, at times acute, at times negligible, that I did not, at some fundamental level, belong. This was true even as I stood there in Peet's, surrounded by the other freakazoids of my adopted hometown; but in Middleburg, the consciousness was so acute as to be dispiriting, even painful.

Driving along the semi-desolate, semi-beautiful boulevards of that city, trying to get a handle on the lives and natures of the mostly white, mostly Anglo-Saxon, mostly Protestant, mostly Republican people who were treating me with such kindness and showing me around their tidy little planet in their great big vehicles, I kept having the thoughts, familiar to anybody who lives in a place as "funky" as Berkeley (i.e., mixed-race, politically progressive, densely urban) that run something like: *Is this my country? Are these my countrymen?* We seemed to have so little in common, to see eye to eye on so few subjects, to find our way into so many conversations where so much could not be said without giving mutual offense or wandering into mutual incomprehension. "I have as much in common with people in Africa or Kyrgyzstan as I did with those folks," I told my daughter. "Maybe less."

But then again, I told her, the only reason I could ever know how wide the gulf was between the Middleburgers and me was because they *were* my countrymen. We were woven, in different patterns, of the same materials of language, economics, politics, and culture. In Africa or Kyrgyzstan, it would have been impossible for me to pick up on the countless nonverbal cues, the artful and artless euphemisms, the cultural and subcultural and pop-cultural references that enabled me to interpret the racial and class biases, the underlying religious and social mores, the styles of dress, the decor of houses, the makes of shoe and automobile, to read all those manifold texts in a way that made the differences between us so plain to me. In other words, the reason I knew we had nothing in common was because we had so much in common.

What was more, I explained to my daughter—the line was moving very slowly—while I was in Middleburg, I got into a couple of conversations, with people whose lives differed almost entirely in their histories and particulars from my own, during which what got revealed to me was not the shared humanity of my Middleburg companion and me but, rather, his or her own fundamental freakazoid nature, the solitary, often forlorn path he or she had wandered through illness, hardship, through the loss of a child and the distortions of consciousness imposed by grief, through a lifelong lonely way of seeing the world. As if the Poesque way of being Alone were indeed the paradoxical essence of that shared humanity. Solitude was our homeland, its population at once one and six billion.

Sometimes you hear—I have said it myself—that if you live in Berkeley or someplace like it, you are "living in a bubble," with the implication that surrounding us here along the banks of Strawberry Creek, or on the shores of San Francisco Bay, is a great uniform mass of normality—scary normality, if you prefer—from which we, to our glory or our shame, more or less flamingly deviate. But the truth is that the bubble is at once much smaller (it is exactly the size of one human being) and much larger than this whole freaky invisible-man-haranguing town (it is as big as this lonely nation, this solitary world).

"So you're saying we're weird," my daughter said, lifting the veil of her hat to take a sip of her decaf gingerbread latte. "I'm weird, is what you're trying to say."

"Yeah, but it's okay," I told her, waving to the lady with the hamster ears. "You have to be weird somewhere. It might as well be here."

This girl started texting my older son. They had known each other since kindergarten but ended up at different middle schools for sixth grade. *Whassup,* was her typical opening gambit; then, *What r u doing?* Sometimes she went on and on, inflating balloon after colored dialogue balloon on the screen of my son's phone.

I couldn't quite get a fix on how the kid felt about it. He seemed flattered, I thought, and a little embarrassed; tickled; annoyed; unable, perhaps, to quite get a fix on how he felt about it himself. For over half his life, this girl had been a source only of that mingled tedium, irritation, and indifference with which little boys tend to regard their female classmates (and vice versa). On the other hand, she was a pretty girl, and their recent separation had no doubt dissolved some of the quasi-incestuous feelings of taboo that previously rendered them unappealing to each other.

My son's response to her text messages, however, was consistent and uniform: He shut her down. *Nothing*, he would text back. *I'm busy. I cant talk right now bye.* My wife and I had attempted to impose some controls on texting as the new behavior came online in the life of our family. No texting while homework remains to be done; no texting during dinner; no texting at all after nine p.m. But even when, by family statute, he was perfectly free to text away, my son would tell this girl that he could not. With other girls in his class, he texted freely, but there was something different in his eyes about this particular relationship, a premonitory tinge of the romantic, which brings me to my point: My son's response to the proffered attention of an attractive young female was, systematically, I would almost say with devotion, to keep his distance. To frost her. He leaped to grab his phone when it quacked; he saw that it was her; he smiled, clearly pleased to hear from her; and then he thumb-typed: *g2g. bye.*

So now, along with everything else—the rules of consent, the imperatives of sexual reciprocity, the fundamental principle of equality—I had to teach him not to be a dick to girls.

Right off, I could see a few potential obstacles to this task. First of all, in order to do the job properly, it might help if I were myself not a dick. And I would like to believe that when it comes to the primary women in my life—wife, daughters, mother—most of the time, and usually but not always for the right reasons, I am a pretty nice guy. Considerate, helpful, willing to show affection, responsive, attentive, loyal, polite, et cetera. But to the extent that this is the case, no credit at all is due to me; it's purely a matter of long years of training, conditioning, and unstinting effort by women—my mother, my first wife, and my current wife of twenty-five years.

I spent the most intensely watchful and empirical years of my life—eleven to seventeen— observing as my mother, a steady and unflappable hand, attempted to steer a sometimes veering course through the treacherous archipelago of men. I can actually remember her telling me with a throb in her voice, three days into a weeklong period of silence and unreturned phone calls that followed some date she thought had gone unusually well, "Promise me that you will never do this to a girlfriend, when you have a girlfriend. If you say that you are going to call her, *you have to call her.*"

I know this made an impression on me—I still remember the conversation forty years later—but I don't think any of my first few serious girlfriends got much benefit from my mother's injunction. Alone, in private, I knew how to treat them with kindness, tenderness, generosity of feeling and expression, but whenever we were in public, in particular among my male friends—and when you are a young man, you are *always* in public, always watching yourself, listening to yourself, audience and judge, checking your behavior against that of the mental list of exemplary men that you have been busy compiling—I was kind of a dick, never serious, never forgiving, never willing to commit to anything that might entangle me in seriousness or the need to forgive. I saw an early episode of *M*A*S*H* recently and was surprised to discover that the character of Hawkeye Pierce—one of my first exemplary men, after my father and Groucho Marx, with both of whom he shared one of the central dickish traits of making a joke out of everything—was not just a total dick but a creep whose primary pastime, apart from alcohol, was unremitting sexual harassment of his female coworkers—or as it was known at the time, rather chillingly, "being a ladies' man." My mother had her share of heartache at the hands of ladies' men.

She set a standard for me, though—keep your promises, be nice, remember the little things, call when you say you will call—and I grew up and got married to a woman who was older than I was and had certain expectations of how she ought and ought not to be treated. It was not just a matter of calling, keeping promises, maintaining the proper form. Even being nice, whatever that means, was insufficient. What loving a grown-up woman required, it turned out, was a kind of fundamental metaphysical shift akin to the move from Jewish to Christian law, from outward obedience and conformity with the commandments, as it were, to the cultivation and maintenance of a righteous soul. I was expected to reach outside myself, beyond the dome and eyeholes of my own skull, imagine the life that was going on inside the head of another human—her fears, wishes, needs, likes and dislikes, longings—and then take these into consideration before I acted. In order to be a man—a real man, by her lights—I must try to imagine what it was like to be a woman. I did my best. We got divorced, and then I got married again, and my daughters were born. And it is in this ongoing business of fathering girls that my root-level dickishness has faced its greatest challenge. With my wife, the process has been a continuing-education course, with those initial adventures in imagining the life inside that other head going far and deep, deeper and farther than with anyone else I've ever known, but somehow my failures with her— the inadvertent public putdowns, the lingering sexist assumptions, the small but crucial promises broken—have never borne the same constant freight of potential disaster as similar lapses with my girls.

Now, I know that when men are called upon to

denounce sexual harassment and rape culture they will often preface or bracket their denunciation with phrases like, "As the father of a daughter . . ." or "Because I care about my daughters . . ." The implication seems to be that unless and until a man has a daughter, he remains incapable of mustering the empathy required to grant women full status as human beings whose rights and integrity must be respected. That's not what I'm saying; in fact, I am saying something almost the opposite: I have been working most of my life, intermittently at first but pretty much constantly since I was twenty-four years old, to imagine myself into the minds and circumstances of the women in my life. But it was not until I had daughters that I fully became aware of—and duly horrified by—the damage that I myself, in my latent dickitude, was capable of inflicting. I remember once taking my older daughter to the hair salon, and when she rose from the chair with a new cut, an asymmetrical bob, going out on a limb a little bit for a fourteen-year-old in her set, saying, "*Daddy?*," seeking my reaction, wanting to know if I thought she looked pretty, I— Well, I don't know what happened. I had been reading a maga-zine, there was some random thought in my head, I looked up, my face must have looked blank, seeing nothing new, nothing remarkable, my mind miles away from where it needed to be right then. *You needed something?* And for a moment her eyes went wide with fear and doubt.

What a dick!

"Beautiful," I told her, but I knew it was too late: she had a crack in her now, fine as a hair but like all cracks irreversible. I was shocked by my own thoughtlessness, and ashamed of it, but the thing I felt most of all was horror. Horror is the only fit response when you are confronted by the full ex-tent of your power to break another human being.

To be a feminist, as a man, it's not enough to ac-knowledge the violence behind the power that you inherited at birth, along with all the entrenched structures, from language to custom to religion, that have been put into place in order to help you maintain it. To be a feminist—defined most sim-ply, so that even an eleven-year-old boy can under-stand it, as the radical assertion that women are human beings—you must repudiate the legacy of violence, and resist those implacable structures of power. But even that's not enough. Even after all the hard work of repudiation and resistance, your privilege will still be there, assigning higher value to your labor, giving your words more time and attention, and basically letting you be as big a dick as you want, whenever and however you please. Against that the only hope is empathy, and for empathy you need to call upon the greatest of all your human inheritances, stronger than violence, able to leap the most entrenched hierarchies in a single bound. To feel the proper horror of the power you have to break someone, you need to use your imagination.

"How come you always blow her off that way?" I said to my son, the next time I saw the little SMS ritual enacted.

I could see the question caught him off guard. He didn't know how to answer it; he probably didn't even know if the question had an answer.

"It probably hurts her feelings," I suggested. "If you think about it."

My son had the sullen grace to acknowledge that this was a possibility.

"I know you don't want to do that," I said. "You're friends. She's a sweet girl."

"She's whatever," my son said.

Not long after that, I suppose, the girl got the message. They never hung out, and she stopped texting him, and I don't remember hearing too much about her at all until my son was about to graduate from high school, and one day her name came up in conversation. My son said that the two of them had lost touch completely, years before, but he had heard through the Berkeley-Oakland high school grapevine that she had pretty much gone off the rails: alcohol, drugs, wild behavior. My son shook his head, looking vaguely pitying, but I didn't hear what I considered to be sufficient sympathy, let alone empathy, in his tone.

"It's probably because you never texted her back," I said, with a straight face, laying on a tone of serious reproach. It was a classic dick move.

I could see him doing the emotional math, charting the butterfly effect of his callousness toward her, all those years ago. His face got very grave, and his eyes widened. For a moment he looked adequately horrified.

"Maybe it is," he said, and I could see that I had put a fine crack in him, too. But that was okay. Sometimes a crack is just what is needed, to let in a little shaft of light.

THE OLD
BALL GAME

didn't want my son to play baseball that spring. I tried to talk him out of it—twice. The first time was in the car, over my shoulder, in an exploratory way, half-joking, with weeks to go until the sign-up deadline for NOLL/SOLL, our local Little League. The second time, just before the fee was due, I actually sat him down. I assumed a grave manner and dwelled on all the reasons I thought he should reconsider. I described the appalling tedium of standing in the outfield, three thousand miles from home plate, cognizant in a vague way that somewhere on the far horizon another nine-year-old was busy striking out swinging, or striking out looking, or walking on three gopher balls and two wild pitches (the league rule being five balls to a walk), or taking his base after getting drilled on the leg or plunked on the helmet.

Batter after batter, inning after inning, week after week, all spring long. I pointed out to him that at the level he would be playing, the games endured six full innings—or three hours, whichever came first. I reminded him that baseball was a hard game to play, a game rooted in failure, glorying in failure (who could forget Merkle's Boner? Not, God knows, me), a game in which you try to hit a hard little ball with a very thin stick. Finally, I broke the news to him—in so many words—that fatherhood is a favorite sideline of assholes, a truth more frequently proved on the baseball diamond than anywhere else. But my son was having none of it. He saw himself out there in the sun, slouched and ready in those white, white pants, with a snappy script name appliquéd to his jersey and a pair of redoubtable cleats. His mother sent in his forms, and we equipped him with a new mitt, and I found myself compelled to expound the gruesome reality of the protective cup.

I suppose I could have simply forbidden him.

That's how my own father handled the situation when I was eight or nine and eager to play. My father is a fan—the original fan, in my world—but that seemed to have no bearing on his feelings about my joining Little League. "You aren't particularly athletic," he informed me. "And the other fathers will disparage you, because they become crazy." I was kind of upset, in fact, as I sat my son down, because I was behaving in a manner that so starkly echoed my father's with me, and I had always resented his having prohibited me from playing Little League.

Like my father, I love baseball, and when I say "love," I'm really talking about a state of being— fandom—with no ready verb of its own. I study baseball like a scholar and a scientist; I dissolve myself in it like a mystic in mystery. In my mind, my history and American history are pegged like currencies to the index of baseball. From the time I was my son's age, I have gone in and out of periods, some lasting years, during which my interest in the game has taken on some of the qualities of obsessive-compulsive disorder, with one in every three thoughts centering on some aspect, large or tiny, of the game and its players. I'm not sure I would go so far as to say that I believe, like *Bull Durham*'s Annie Savoy, in the Church of Baseball, but I live in its House; I shelter in its Friendly Confines. It has always seemed regrettable, therefore, that I never got to play the game at the organized level. Pickup games, schoolyard and backyard and street ball, yes. But I have never worn a real baseball uniform. I have no illusions, I hasten to add, that I would have done honor to said uniform, or even managed not to embarrass myself, but at times I have regretted that lost opportunity—and blamed my father for that regret.

So I wasn't going to tell my son he couldn't play.

Besides, I reasoned, he might like it. He might even love it. He might very well prove me wrong. I like it when my children prove me wrong; I enjoy the sensation, though not quite as much, perhaps, as I enjoy being right. I was going to be surprised if my son enjoyed cooling his cleats in the Kamchatka of center right, or if he managed to collect a few solid base hits, or if he passed an entire season without being exposed to any stark assholery from the fathers at the game. I guess you could say that when I gave in and said he could play this year, I was hoping to be surprised.

No such luck: He hated every minute of it. By the second game of the season he was pleading to be allowed to miss practice, to skip games, to quit. Like the Milwaukee Braves on the days not assigned to Spahn or Sain, my son prayed for rain, and often enough, that rainy spring, his prayers were answered. When it didn't rain, he and I would drive down to a grim diamond in West Oakland, scraped out of a chance gap between a decommissioned army base and a storage yard for ISO containers, and sometimes I would sit with the team in the chain-link dugout on the rickety two-by-six that served as a bench, keeping score.

Keeping score is an emblematic pleasure of being a baseball fan. The craft of scorekeeping unites the taking of field notes, the inscribing of occult alphabets, the chronicling of history, and the repetition of an uncontrollable tic. It is also, like fandom itself, the gift of my father, an art he imparted in the stands at Memorial Stadium, during Game 1 of the 1971 American League playoffs between Baltimore and Oakland. There is no surer way for a spectator to keep his or her mind on a game than to track it with a pencil on a scorecard, and since I was going to be no help at all to my son's team as a coach on the field, I was happy to have some way to contribute.

But keeping score for yourself in the stands, with a Coke between your knees and all of baseball history spread out before you in the green splendor of the grounds, is one thing. No one depends on your accuracy, neatness, or skill. You might as well be counting the pigeons wheeling in the grandstand or ticking off the progress of the shadows as they grow long across the outfield. The scorecards that I filled out for my son's team, on the other hand, were official documents to be registered and recorded with the league. The number of throws by each young pitcher, in particular, was to be monitored so that nobody's arm got ruined. If I missed a sacrifice, or lost track of a run batted in, it was as if it never happened at all. That made it hard to relax and enjoy the game, though I noticed that when I was there in the dugout with the team, my son seemed to hate the game a little less. But he never stopped begging to be allowed to drop out.

I wouldn't let him quit. I forced him to attend Thursday practices and show up for the endless Saturday games. Even when he cried. Even though I found that I hated Little League, too, and for a reason I hadn't considered in trying to warn him away, a reason I would not have the heart to try to explain.

My prior exposure to "youth baseball" was on Vashon Island, Washington, during the spring of 1990, when, as a favor to a ten-year-old friend, I served as scorekeeper for his Mustang League team. It was a talented team that won a lot of games, and the experience of Little League struck me as positive on the whole, though every so often there was trouble with an asshole dad. But those Vashon boys were a little wild, in the way that I remembered myself having been wild as a kid. When they were not at school or Scouts or on the baseball field, they went out into the woods and the empty lots, and rode their bikes to the ends of the island. They got lost, and blew things up, and set things on fire, and fell into all kinds of mud. It made sense, it evened things out somehow, for them to submit themselves a few days a week to regulation play.

My son didn't have a sandlot to repair to on a Sunday afternoon. Nobody ever came by with a glove and a Wiffle ball to see if he wanted to hit some, at least not without complicated arrangements having been made beforehand by the parents. He had no idea that a baseball game was something that could just happen to a kid, spontaneous as a fever, that it could be disorganized, random, open-ended, played according to quirky and variant rules, with manhole covers and car fenders for bases and a mean old lady for a color commentator.

What I came to dislike about Little League that spring was not the regulation per se, or the fathers—whose consciousness had generally been raised at least a little bit—or the tedium, or the low quality of play, or the pain of watching my son strike out a lot. It was the way I got reminded, every game, that this was the world my children lived in: the world in which the wild watershed of childhood had been brought fully under control of the adult Corps of Engineers. Looking at my son and the other boys on his team, I felt the way I do sometimes when I look at a poodle and think about wolves. I was never a wolf as a kid, but I used to chase cars, and dig escape tunnels under fences, and run around for days on end without a leash.

It stopped raining and my son played out his games, and the season ended, and we were both relieved. I told him I was proud of him for finishing what he'd started, for fulfilling his commitment to his teammates and his coaches, for hanging in there at the plate, for getting his glove down once or twice to stop a grounder that seemed likely to get by him. But when I looked at baseball now, I sensed a gathering darkness in my view.

The truth was that I had been suffering for a number of years from a deepening case of baseball depression. This is an ailment little talked about but which I believe must be fairly widespread among lovers of the game. So much of what we call baseball is really our attachment to the past, to our own histories and baseball's—as if there were any difference between the two. One of the seminal baseball books is an oral history of early professional ball called *The Glory of Their Times,* and that title pretty much summarizes the retrospective bent of fandom. An educated baseball fan over a certain age fights a lifelong battle against the dangerous tendency to lapse into gloom about the present state of the game, of its players, and of the world they seem, on bad days, to represent. And that has been true for at least the past fifty years.

Watching my boy live his life between the lines, comparing his constricted field of play to the relatively unbounded one that I remembered, I felt myself giving in to this same style of thinking. I was tired of the steroid scandals, of the ballparks that changed their names with every corporate collapse or merger, of salary arbitration, of trying to keep track of the insane permutations of team rosters from season to season, of losing my favorites to free agency every year, of cupidity and stupidity among the owners and players, of rock and hip-hop songs being blasted at the park, of five-man rotations and setup men and pitchers who couldn't lay down a bunt. I missed the old dominance of the great African-American ballplayers I grew up with: the flash and speed and power. I missed the dynastic infields, the double-play combinations that endured for years. I missed the musical reign of the organ and the moments of strange silence that used to settle over a ballpark between innings or batters, even when the stands were packed.

I revile all codgers, coots, and *alter kockers* with their retrograde agendas, and it pained me to find myself among them. I tried to remind myself of the ugly system that preceded free agency, of the statistically provable superiority of modern play to that of the glory times, of the undisputed beauty that has resulted, thanks to the demands of expansion, from the increasing presence of international players in the game. But sometimes it seemed like it might be better simply to stop thinking about baseball entirely.

Then one day a few weeks after the Little League season ended, I was watching San Francisco play Anaheim on television. My wife was out of town, and I had put the kids to bed, and Matt Cain, then a young pitcher for the Giants, was taking a no-hitter into the sixth. Right as I was wishing there were somebody to enjoy the kid's performance with me, my elder daughter came in, having finished the novel she was reading (*Watership Down*, for those who are keeping score). She curled up on the couch with me and got totally sucked into the game. She asked a lot of questions: What is a no-hitter? A shutout? A perfect game? Why is the runner standing so far from the bag at first? What is the catcher saying to the pitcher when he trudges out to the mound for a visit?

It wasn't the first time my daughter had watched a game with me; far from it. But it was the first time she seemed to understand enough of baseball to know that she didn't understand; and that, of course, is the beginning of wisdom, and of fandom, too.

I wondered, sitting with my eleven-year-old

daughter smushed companionably against me, employing me as furniture in a way that I never would have dreamed of attempting with my father, if I had somehow spoiled baseball for my son and me by laying too much emphasis on it as something for fathers and sons to share, if my daughter had been just waiting all these years for me to admit her onto the playing field, or if maybe I was mistaken in my memories. Maybe I hadn't really come to love baseball, to fully understand it, until I was nearly twelve, like her.

I did my best to answer, and I think I answered well. It was an exciting game, one that introduced her not only to the key concepts of the no-hitter and the young phenom but also to that of the pesky little spark plug, in the person of Anaheim's Chone Figgins, who broke up the no-hitter in the top of the eighth with a line-drive hit to center, and scored the Angels' only run against Matt Cain with some aggressive base-running. She was moved by the ovation Cain received on leaving the game. She cringed and gasped and cheered her way through Armando Benítez's successful effort to save the game for Cain in the bottom of the ninth.

"That was fun," she said when it was over and the Giants had won.

"It was," I said. "A lot of fun."

"I want to watch another one. Is there a game tomorrow night?"

I said there was. There would be a whole summer's worth of games, every summer, for the rest of our lives.

One Saturday when I was twelve or thirteen, I went to the T-shirt counter at McCrory's dime store, in the Columbia mall, and had them print me up a custom one, using heat-transfer letters and a steam press. I chose a light blue cotton-poly blend; the letters were dark blue, almost purple, made from some fuzzy iron-on stuff, in a functional sans-serif typeface like you might employ to put your last name on the back of your baseball jersey, which was probably the use for which the letters had been intended. I think I may have been inspired to communicate with the world in this way by the example of a then-well-known photograph of the comedian Chevy Chase, in which he was shown wearing a T-shirt that said YES IT'S MY REAL NAME. I went in kind of a different direction, though. My shirt said LIBERTINE.

I find this memory somewhat surprising. It is a clear memory: I remember the adhesive-tape smell of the letters, the slick clingy feel of the shirt, my reflection in the bathroom mirror, the word reversed, my bespectacled face grinning from ear to ear. I remember enduring all kinds of puzzled looks, mispronunciations (people liked to rhyme it with "*valentine*") and questions, chief among which, of course, was "What the hell is a libertine?"

I was only too happy to provide a definition. "It means a freethinker," I would say, giving what I knew to be the word's decidedly secondary sense. I don't remember if I ever offered the primary meaning, which is, according to the *New Oxford American Dictionary* on my Macintosh, "a person, esp. a man, who behaves without moral principles or a sense of responsibility, esp. in sexual matters." But I was fully aware of this lurid aspect of the word. I had encountered *"libertine"* in some work of musty pornography, one of a number of self-important, intellectual-looking Grove Press Black

Cat paperbacks—Marquis de Sade, John Cleland, Pierre Louÿs, the ever popular Anonymous—that my parents half-heartedly concealed in the book-case headboard of their bed. I knew all of its inter-esting synonyms: *"roué," "rake," "lothario," "satyr."* But I never would have gone to McCrory's and asked the lady to print one of those words on a shirt ("rake" in particular). Something about *"libertine,"* that Latinate dactyl chiming at its finish like a bell, stirred me, caught my fancy, and persuaded me to adopt it as a proper or at least a hopeful label for myself.

Looking back, as I say, I'm surprised by this choice, or perhaps it would be more accurate to say that I'm surprised by the memory of the person who made it. First of all, I was not, in fact, a libertine. When it came to sex, all I had ever done was masturbate, with the ready assistance of that semi-concealed library, an activity that raised no questions in my mind of moral principle or re-sponsibility. Furthermore, my sense of principle was strong, in the usual way of young teenagers. The world was all justice and injustice, fairness

and unfairness, offense and outrage and hypocri-
sies to be scorned. I might not have been the most
responsible kid in the world, but I cooked dinner
and walked the dog, did my homework without be-
ing told, visited my grandparents. As for being a
freethinker—this was, like, 1976. Punk rock was
experiencing its birth pangs. My parents smoked
pot. *Five Easy Pieces* was a big-studio Hollywood
movie. Freethinking was orthodoxy. A true liber-
tine of the time would have been obliged to repu-
diate stale convention by submitting to some rigid
doctrine, say, or by only listening to the kind of
Dixieland jazz they played on Main Street, U.S.A.,
at Disney World.

The thing that surprises me the most, however,
is that in retrospect I appear to have felt confident
or comfortable enough, in the eyes of the world,
to wear that shirt—many times—in the halls of
Ellicott City Middle School. When I consider the
boy I was in seventh grade, which, frankly, I try
to do as seldom as possible, I tend to see a shy,
persecuted, *Space: 1999*–watching, bespectacled
über-nerd slinking as unobtrusively through the

hallways as possible, living in constant fear of having his glasses broken or his books dumped. Pity for oneself as a child feels more pardonable than pity for the current model and is almost as satisfying. And narratives of one's former loserhood are always, to a degree, a form of self-flattery, since, like the origin tales of costumed heroes, they proceed by drawing a contrast between Before and After, and take for granted the presence, in the unformed embryonic superbeing, of seeds of greatness.

But this matter of the LIBERTINE T-shirt would seem to cast doubt on that old origin tale. Because whatever my intentions might have been in choosing that particular text, the real message of my T-shirt, as poorly encrypted as my parents' library of Enlightenment and Victorian pornography, was *"Ask me about my T-shirt!"* I was exposing myself, willingly, to the attention of others, and furthermore to the possibility, admittedly slight among that particular body of students, that somebody might know what "libertine" actually meant, and would spread the word that I enjoyed, say, sodomizing chambermaids and valets while wearing a leather mask. By testing the limits of my classmates' and teachers' knowledge and intelligence, daring them to be as smart, or at least as well read in fancy smut as I was, I was flirting with disaster, publicly. And that makes me appear to have been not only confident as a twelve-year-old but even cocky. Or maybe, as my wife suggests, I just couldn't help myself; I was not in control of my signification. In wearing that crazy T-shirt, I was fulfilling not my hidden destiny as a freethinker but simply collaborating with my oppressors in singling me out for abuse, evolving the coloration appropriate to my ecological niche. I was not Napoleon; I was Napoleon Dynamite.

I first found myself recalling this business of the LIBERTINE T-shirt as I watched my older son struggling, in so many ways, against the crushing orthodoxy of middle school (so aptly named!), against the opinions and strictures of his classmates (nice kids, taken individually). I had forgotten how socially repressive twelve-year-olds really are, how closed-minded, as *anti*-libertine as the

Calvinism to which we owe our present notion of the word. In seventh grade, at Hanukkah, my son asked for, and received, a peacoat. It was a classic number, navy blue, double-breasted wool, great big plastic buttons stamped—oh, the coolness!—with little anchors. We got it from an online army-navy store. It had a quilted lining, and when he wore it on a gray East Bay afternoon, with an extra-long scarf striped in muted colors wrapped around his neck, and his hair cut in a late-'65, early-'66 Small Faces shag, he looked terrific. Stylish and lanky and handsome; and warm. Over Christmas break he wore it constantly, and to everything he said and did, with that scarf blowing out behind him, there was a whiff of oracular *Blonde on Blonde* cool. He did not so much walk around in it as *lope*.

Then one chilly January morning when the school carpool arrived, he ran out the door wearing only his old zippered Volcom hoodie. "I left it at school," he explained when I asked him where the peacoat was. He was forgetful, and I am forgetful, and there followed a week or two of cold weather, and every day he braved it in his hoodie. And then

one day I happened to notice the peacoat hanging
in the hall closet. For another week thereafter I
reminded him to wear it—the weather had turned
even colder—and he always said the same thing:
"It doesn't look good with these jeans." This state-
ment seemed not to depend on the cut or color of
the jeans he was wearing. Finally, I got the point:
He wasn't going to be wearing his peacoat to school
anymore. I asked him why, and even before the
flicker of pain came and went across his features, I
knew—I remembered—the answer.

"Did somebody make fun of you in your coat?"

"I look like a mushroom."

"You do not."

"I look all emo."

"Oh, come on. You look so cool in that coat."

But then I dropped it, for I knew that there
are few sentences more utterly devoid of mean-
ing than than those in which your parents assert
your coolness. I remember only too well how it
felt, when I was his age, to find myself caught up
in the mystifying tangle of secret legislation that
determined which clothes and styles were cool

and which were hopeless. One Monday you would show up for school in your Levi's, or (in my case, alas) your stiff reinforced-knee Sears Toughskins, and discover that over the weekend everyone but you appeared to have received a memorandum informing them that Britannia was the sole acceptable brand of blue jeans. Or you would be informed by a panel of experts (whose accreditation appeared to derive from the same mysterious authority that had sent out the Britannia memo) that your new pair of sneakers, with their bright red plimsoll lines, in which you had passed an entire Sunday afternoon at the basketball hoop over the garage hopefully noting improvements in your vertical leap, your turnaround jump shot, and your overall élan, belonged irrevocably to that dreaded class of footwear known, in the Baltimore area at that time, as "fish heads." At my son's age, kids seem to be wired with an unerring instinct, even a yearning, for that perfection of conformity, as inexplicable and wondrous in its way as the ability of a thousand birds all to make the same abrupt turn to the left at the same instant, known by its celebrants and detractors alike as *"fashion,"* a word whose literal, original meaning is "a behavior engaged in by a group."

So I got his old serviceable ski jacket out of the closet—it was only a little short at the wrists—and wished that we could just take him out of school entirely for the next few years, travel the world, read good books, learn how to program our computers. Just pole-vault him clear over the whole middling middle school experience, so that he would alight, more competent, more well-rounded, and surer of who he was, on the doorstep of high school, having been given the opportunity to try on and discard as many coats and identities as he cared to try, without fear of ridicule or shame. But I guess we are too conformist for that.

And then one week toward the end of eighth grade, when I picked him up from school (I had missed seeing him in the morning), he came out to the car wearing the burgundy velour blazer and the blue-and-white-plaid ultra-bell-bottom slacks that had constituted his Halloween costume a couple of years earlier—he'd gone as Austin Powers—over a black Rush T-shirt, to whose collar he had clipped a green tartan bow tie. He looked preposterous. He looked splendid.

"Wow," I said. "Where's your shirt?" There had been a vintage seventies tuxedo shirt to complete the Austin Powers effect, I remembered, lemon yellow, foaming at the bodice with black-edged ruffles.

"Couldn't find it."

He got in the car, and we drove for a little while, and then I said, "So what did the kids have to say about your look?"

He shrugged. "Nothing. I don't know. Whatever."

Oh, well, I thought. *So much for that.* Tomorrow it would be back to the brand-name skatewear that was the only acceptable fashion for the boys of his set. At least he kept *trying* to express himself, his real self, as motley and inchoate for now as the outfit he was wearing. And maybe that was part of the purpose of middle school: to give you something to work against, to press upon, as you attempted to *fashion* a self from the lump of contradictory impulses and emotions and paradigms that your mind and your culture presented.

I put my hand on his shoulder. "You look great," I told him.

The next morning when he came down to breakfast, he was wearing the fabulous yellow shirt and a face that said, *"Nothing, I don't know. Whatever."*

The peacoat, I thought, had a little room in the shoulders. It might still fit him next winter, if he felt like putting it on.

You want to be a doctor, too?" the patient asks me, pushing up his left shirtsleeve the way my father has instructed him to do. He is an older man with jowls and a silvery crew cut, wearing a short-sleeved shirt and a necktie and pinned to a kitchen chair by the boulder of his abdomen. The tap drips water into a cup in the kitchen sink. The smell of the patient's dinner lingers, raw meat and fat against cast iron.

When I don't immediately reply to his question, the patient looks up at my father, who has come to the patient's home this evening to conduct an insurance physical. My father reaches into his black bag for his sphygmomanometer, unrolls the cuff, and uncoils the rubber tubing. Like many young doctors not long out of medical school, he supplements his income doing these in-home exams. After putting in a full day as a pediatrician at the Phoenix Indian Hospital, where he has been posted by the U.S. Public Health Service, he comes home just long enough to shower and shave for the second time that day, change his shirt and tie, grab a quick bite. Then he heads back out to perform one or more exams for one of the big insurance companies, often taking me with him. Sometimes, as has happened earlier tonight, we forgo dinner at home and stop at a favorite restaurant, a Mexican place called Ricardo's.

"Cute little guy," the patient says to my father in a confidential tone, then calls to me, parked in a corner on another kitchen chair, "You want to be a doctor, eh? Just like your daddy?" Trying again, maybe I didn't hear him the first time.

I take my sphygmomanometer out of my black bag. Unlike my father's, with its rubberized canvas cuff, sturdy squeeze bulb, and steel-and-glass gauge, mine is made entirely of brightly colored thin plastic, like my Taylor hammer, my otoscope, my syringe, and the stethoscope that I wear dangling like a pendant necklace, the way my father does, with the earpieces pincering my neck. My black bag is plastic, too, a flimsy, lightweight affair with none of the pachyderm heft and dignity of my father's. The mouth of my father's bag opens and closes smoothly on the hinges of a secret armature, clasped by a heavy brass tongue that slides home with a satisfying click. Mine pops open when you flip a plastic tab that has begun to shear loose and will soon snap off. A vial of candy "pills" was the sole advantage my black bag possessed over my father's, but I have long since prescribed and administered them to myself. The empty vial rolls around at the bottom of the bag.

I hunch my shoulders, racked with the dreadful hope that the patient might be about to invite me to come over and "check" his blood pressure. I squeeze the bulb of my gimcrack instrument; I don't feel that the word *"cute"* suits either me or the gravity of the situation. On my previous outings, a few of the patients have allowed me to pretend to stick them with my needleless needle and to hear their hearts beat through my sham stethoscope. There is nothing I want more than for my presence to be taken seriously, and nothing guaranteed

to render me more painfully aware of my fraud-
ulence. The truth is, I don't especially want to
be a doctor when I grow up. Or, rather, I've come
to understand that while my presence at these
house calls may be cute, or amusing, it is in no
way *promising*: I know I am not really cut out for
the job.

Based partly on direct observation and partly on
his tales of his own medical prowess, I have already
formed the impression that my father is an excel-
lent doctor. Though he will in other ways disap-
point, disillusion, or unfavorably surprise me over
the coming decades, this impression will stand. In
his hospital tales, my father stars as a first-rate di-
agnostician with near-Holmesian powers to infer
rare or easily missed pathologies from the slightest
of symptoms. As a small boy, I have no way (and
no desire) to disprove these claims; I have to take
his word for them.* But I have been an eyewitness

---

*Though I had observed that whenever a patient on a TV show
like *Marcus Welby, M.D.*, or *Ben Casey* presented with odd
symptoms, my father always made what proved to be the cor-
rect diagnosis long before the first commercial break.

to a number of displays of my father's other re-
markable skill as a doctor, one that mysteriously is
never the focus of his storytelling: an uncommon
gift for reassurance, for making his patients feel
that he registers and sympathizes with their pain
or discomfort and their anxieties about treatment
itself; that he is really listening to them, really see-
ing them. Later in life I will encounter and come
to understand other self-centered people capable
of great feats of empathy only within certain nar-
row yet powerful contexts—while writing novels,
say—but for the moment I cling to the misguided
hope that the ray of his compassionate attention
will one day be directed toward me.*

Both his bedside manner and his diagnostic

---

*Unless I was gravely ill or seriously injured—and I was al-
most never either of those things—I didn't even rate the bed-
side manner. My father's response when I cut a finger, stubbed
a toe, twisted an ankle, or fell off my bicycle never varied: *We'll
have to amputate.* When a suture or two was probably called
for, he made do with butterflying a pair of Band-Aids; when I
fell off a stair railing and broke my arm, he set it with an ACE
bandage and a flat plastic tool for scraping the ice off our wind-
shield.

chops depend, however, on my father's funda-
mental superpower, which is that, as far as I can
tell, he knows everything. His memory is pro-
found, his command of facts sweeping and indis-
criminate.

He knows the genealogies of English kings, the
birth names of all five Marx Brothers, the Köchel
numbers of the major works of Mozart, the bat-
ting averages of the top ten all-time hitters in both
leagues, the differing effects on Superman of the
various colors of Kryptonite. He has read every
important book, seen every classic film, listened to
every great symphony. When we listen to classical
music in the car, he whistles ostentatiously along
with even the most complex and atonal themes. He
remembers people's names, details, and particulars.
When examining an anxious young patient, he is
able to call not simply on large swaths of medical
knowledge but on a disarming command of pop-
cultural information that helps put both children
and their parents at ease: He knows the name of
Underdog's archenemy (Simon Bar Sinister) and of
Barbie's little sister (Skipper); he keeps up with the

intricacies of daytime soap operas and baseball box scores.

There is really no point, I have already decided, in even trying to pass myself off as a doctor, a would-be doctor, or a pint-size future version of my father. No matter how hard I try, and this is an assessment my father seems to share, I will never know as much as he does or be as intelligent as he is. *You are a very smart boy,* he has informed me, a few times now, after I came out with some unexpected fact or precocious bit of perception. *Of course, you'll never be as smart as me,* he always adds, smiling in a way that seems apologetic and mocking at the same time.

"Following in your footsteps?" the patient says, trying my father again, talking a lot, nervous, perhaps.

At first my father doesn't answer. When I'm older, he will explain that he used to bring me along with him because the presence of a small child was an icebreaker for anxious patients in a potentially awkward social situation, but in hindsight this strikes me as improbable. It strikes me now that he may simply have wanted my company, or felt guilty about working evenings after having spent his whole day in the company of other people's children. Or maybe he just liked to show me off, or show off to me. He had schooled me, for example, to name the presidents in order from Washington through to LBJ. Often during the house calls, he would call on me at some point to perform this, or one of the other circus acts of memory—U.S. state capitals, Canadian provincial capitals—in which he found me a willing pony. These may not have broken any ice, but they unquestionably reflected well on his own abilities, both as a rememberer himself and as a skilled trainer of children.

"Like father, like son?" the patient adds helpfully.

My father has fitted the earpieces of his stethoscope to his ears. He slides its diaphragm under the blood pressure cuff. One eyebrow arched, he listens to the patient's pulse with an expression of calm intensity that to this day remains the badge, in my imagination, of an engaged and curious mind. A few years later I will watch Leonard Nimoy, as

Mr. Spock, look up from his scanner on the bridge of the USS *Enterprise*, and catch the echo of my father's face.

"I don't know about that," my father replies finally, uncuffing the patient's forearm. "He might be a little too squeamish."

This is a new word to me, but I grasp its meaning immediately. Doctors stick people with needles, cut them open, take their blood, lay bare their bones and organs. Inevitably, doctors—even doctors with gentle and reassuring manners, like my father—inflict pain.

"Is that right?" The patient looks at me. (In my recollection of that night, I see from his expression that I have disappointed him or let him down, but maybe what I saw on the patient's face was only bafflement: If I didn't want to grow up to be a doctor, then why was I in the man's kitchen at seven o'clock on a weeknight, with a doctor's bag?) "So, what *do* you want to be?"

I think back to the subject of conversation between my father and me in our booth at Ricardo's earlier this evening. Ricardo's is the only Mexican restaurant I have ever been to at this point in my life (Mexican restaurants being nowhere as commonplace then as now), and so I have no point of comparison, but decades later, living in California, I will come to understand that Ricardo's was a Mexican restaurant of the old school: half-elegant, red Naugahyde and dark wood trimmed in wrought iron, a throwback even then to an era when white people still thought of Mexico as an exotic land inhabited by cacti, burros, men in sombreros, and Lupe Vélez. For my father, a Brooklyn boy, there was still something exotic in 1967 about tacos and tamales. To me, there was a solemnity in the iron and wood interior, the chill air, the shadowed booths. Meals there took on an adult air of significance. At the front of the restaurant, the cashier sat behind an old-school glass display case well stocked with candy, gum, cigarettes, and especially cigars laid out in their ornate and colorful boxes that depicted great generals and queens, gods of ancient Egypt, Indians in full regalia.

Over our dinner tonight my father remarked that when he was a boy, almost every decent restaurant had featured a cabinet of wonders of this kind; now almost none of them did. This observation prompted me to ask him other questions about the world of his boyhood, long ago. He told me about the elevated trains of Brooklyn, about the all-day programs at his local movie theater: a newsreel, a cartoon, a serial, a comedy short, the B picture, and, finally, the A picture, all for a dime. He talked about comic books, radio dramas, *Astounding* magazine, and the stories they had told: rocket-powered heroes, bug-eyed monsters, mad scientists bent on using science to rule the world. He described to me how he had saved box tops from cold cereals like Post Toasties, and redeemed them by mail for Junior G-Man badges or cardboard Flying Fortresses that carried payloads of black marbles. He told me about playing games like potsy, stickball, handball, ringolevio, and for the first but by no means the last time, about an enchanted pastry called a charlotte russe, a rosette of whipped cream on a disk of sponge cake served in a scalloped paper cup, topped with a maraschino cherry. He described having spent weeks in the cellar of his Flatbush apartment building as a young teenager, trying and failing, with some mail-order chemicals, five pounds of kosher salt, and a lantern battery, to re-create "the original recipe for life on earth," as given in the pages of *Astounding*.

In the air-conditioned red darkness of Ricardo's, across from the cigar case, the past and the future became alloyed in my imagination: magic and science, heroes and villains, brick-and-steel Brooklyn and the chromium world of tomorrow. My father, an inveterate list maker, rattled off the names of games, trains, and radio shows, stopping to give little in the way of description, yet it all came to life for me, as gaudy and vivid and fragrant as those boxes of cigars. Beyond the minimal contours that my father hastily sketched—we had a patient to get to—some quirk in me, in the wiring of my brain or the capability of my heart, enabled me to ride the bare rails of his memory into the past. In my head, in what I was just coming to understand without even putting a name to it, as my *imagination*, I felt that I was or had been present on Flatbush Avenue at the passing of his vivid, vanished childhood. I did not know how I was managing the trick or what it might be good for—I was not even neces-sarily aware that I was doing it—but I knew imme-diately that it was *my* secret superpower.

Fair enough: So, what *do* I want to be? How to answer the patient, who is now taking long slow breaths, in through the nose, out through the mouth, as the drum of the stethoscope makes checkers moves across his back. I put away the plastic sphyg-momanometer and snap the flimsy clasp of my counterfeit black bag. Let my father be the doctor—when I grow up, I want to tell the patient, I will be-come a guy who gets to live inside and outside of his own mind and body at the same time, traveling, without moving, into other worlds, other places, other lives. But I don't know quite how to put it, or exactly what kind of work the proper deployment of my superpower might suit me for or entail.

"I'm probably going to be a mad scientist," I announce to the patient, to my father, and, a little wonderingly, to myself. "And make the original recipe for creating life on earth."

Fifty years on, though my father has long since re-tired from regular practice both as a doctor and as a father, I'm still chasing after that recipe for life and still, four times a father myself, doing part-time work as a son. At this point, to be honest, being my father's son is less than a sideline; it's more like a hobby, one of a number of pastimes acquired early, pursued with intensity, laid aside, and then only intermittently, over the years, resumed: origami, cartooning, model building, being a base-ball fan, being a son. I think of my father at least once every day, try (but fail) to call him once a week, and, as required, afford regular access to his grandchildren. Beyond that, the contours of the job turn vague and history-haunted. Outside the safe zone of our telephone calls, with their set menu of capsule film and book reviews, amateur political punditry, and two-line status reports on the other members of our respective households, the terri-tory of our father-and-sonhood is shadowed by the usual anger, disappointment, and failure, strewn with the bones of old promises and lies.

Strange how a relationship—*the* relationship—that I understand as truly primal, as foundational, for good and ill, to the construction of my self, my worldview, my art, and my approach to being a father, should for decades now have consisted in and subsisted on a studied avoidance of any but the most ancillary and weightless interactions!

And yet it's in my capacity as his son that I board a flight from Oakland to Portland, Oregon, home to my father for the past seven years, traveling on a full-fare last-minute ticket, hoping that he's still alive when I get there. The day before yesterday my father fell so ill, so suddenly, that he consented—for the first time that anyone can remember—to being hospitalized. *A hospital,* he always says, *is the worst place to be sick.* He's home again for now, but I have been given reason to believe that if I want to see him again—and, of course, at the moment, seeing him is all I want to do—I'd better not hesitate. When the plane lands, I take my phone out of airplane mode with a sense of dread and dramatic irony, but there's no fatal text message. I rush over from PDX to the apartment downtown, messaging with my stepmother and my half brother all the way.

When I called to say that I would be flying up to see him, my father made the expected but un-expectedly feeble attempt to dismiss my urgency as baseless and my visit as gratuitous, but as soon as I walk into the bedroom, I can tell he is happy to have me there. Although he seems to be out of danger for the time being (and will make a decent recovery from what eventually gets diagnosed as a nasty combination of stroke, kidney failure, and acute bronchitis), he freely acknowledges that he just came very near to death.

"The day before yesterday was bad," he admits. "According to your stepmother, I was raving. Saying a lot of things that didn't make sense."

"How could she tell the difference?"

"That's exactly what I said."

I lie down beside him on my stepmother's side of the king-size bed. The flat-screen television mounted on the opposite wall is tuned to TCM, which happens to be showing a film I first saw with my father, when I was eleven or twelve: Fritz Lang's *Metropolis*. Every few minutes my father is racked by spasms of gnarly-sounding coughing that have left his voice a ragged whisper; if he taxes it beyond speaking a sentence or two, whatever he says dissolves into a fit of hacking and gasping for breath. It seems best, therefore, to avoid conversation entirely. We lie there for a long time, contemplating Lang's quaint dystopia as it silently unravels. In the fifty-four years of our mutual acquaintance, I cannot remember our ever having sustained so prolonged a silence in each other's company.

It turns out to be not the worst way to spend an hour of your life. But after a while I find myself thinking about the conversation we aren't having. I start having it with him in my head.

This is a great film, but *M* is the masterpiece.
I just saw it again: incredible. But what about *Dr. Mabuse*?
A great film, too, but I think you have to give it to *M*. Have you ever seen *Hangmen Also Die!*?
A long time ago, I never really cared for the Hollywood films. You know she was a Nazi.
Thea von Harbou? Yeah.*
Lang's mother was Jewish. His wife was a member of the Nazi Party.
Hey, that would make a great sitcom.

---

*Von Harbou, screenwriter of *Metropolis*, was married to Fritz Lang from 1922 to 1933.

The cadence, the tenor, the content of the conversation are all so readily accessible to my mind's ear that they come unbidden, as clearly and freely as if we're speaking the words aloud. I wonder how long it has been since the last time we did this, just lie around in the middle of the afternoon watching a great movie together. I decide that the answer is probably something in the neighborhood of forty years. And then, equally unbidden, comes the thought: *This is how it will be when he is gone.* I will be lying on a bed somewhere, watching *Citizen Kane,* or *A Night at the Opera,* or *The Man with the X-Ray Eyes,* or some other film that became beloved to me through my father's own loving intervention, and even though he won't be there anymore, I will still be watching it with him. I will hear his voice then the way I am hearing it now, in my head, that instrument set up and tuned to his signal long ago, angled to catch the flow of my father's information, his opinions, all the million great and minor things he knows. After he's gone into that all too imaginable darkness—soon enough now—I will have found another purpose for the superpower that my father discovered in me, one evening half a century ago, riding the solitary rails of my imagination into our mutual story, into the future we envisioned and the history we actually accumulated; into the vanished world that once included him.

"Little Man" was originally published in *GQ* under the title "My Son, the Prince of Fashion." "Adventures in Euphemism" was originally published on atlantic.com, under the title "The Unspeakable, in Its Jammies." "The Bubble People" (under the title "One of Us"), "Against Dickitude," "The Old Ball Game," and "Be Cool or Be Cast Out" were originally published in *Details*.

ABOUT THE AUTHOR

MICHAEL CHABON is the bestselling and Pulitzer Prize–winning author of *The Mysteries of Pittsburgh, A Model World, Wonder Boys, Werewolves in Their Youth, The Amazing Adventures of Kavalier & Clay, Summerland, The Final Solution, The Yiddish Policemen's Union, Maps & Legends, Gentlemen of the Road, Manhood for Amateurs, Telegraph Avenue, Moonglow,* and the picture book *The Astonishing Secret of Awesome Man.* He lives in Berkeley, California, with his wife, the novelist Ayelet Waldman, and their children.

BOOKS BY MICHAEL CHABON

THE FINAL SOLUTION
A Story of Detection

In *The Amazing Adventures of Kavalier and Clay*, prose magician Michael Chabon conjured the golden age of comic books, interwining history, legend and story-telling verve. In *The Final Solution*, he has condensed his boundless vision to create a short, suspenseful tale of compassion and wit that re-imagines the classic 19th-century detective story.

THE MYSTERIES OF PITTSBURGH
A Novel

The enthralling debut from bestselling novelist Michael Chabon is a penetrating narrative of complex friendships, father-son conflicts, and the awakening of a young man's sexual identity.

THE YIDDISH POLICEMEN'S UNION
A Novel

At once a gripping whodunit, a love story, an homage to 1940s noir, and an exploration of the mysteries of exile and redemption, *The Yiddish Policemen's Union* is a novel only Michael Chabon could have written.

MANHOOD FOR AMATEURS
The Pleasures and Regrets of a Husband, Father, and Son

Michael Chabon "takes [his] brutally observant, unfailingly honest, marvelously human gaze and turns it on his own life" (*Time*) in the *New York Times* bestselling memoir *Manhood for Amateurs*.

MAPS AND LEGENDS
Reading and Writing Along the Borderlands

Map and Legends is Chabon's first book-length foray into nonfiction, with 16 essays, some previously published. Several of these essays are defenses of the author's work in genre literature (such as science fiction, fantasy, and comics), while others are more autobiographical, explaining how the author came to write several of his most popular works.

BOOKS BY MICHAEL CHABON

TELEGRAPH AVENUE
A Novel

The *New York Times* bestseller, now available in paperback—a big-hearted, exhilarating novel exploring the profoundly intertwined lives of two Oakland families.

MOONGLOW
A Novel

Following on the heels of his *New York Times* bestselling novel *Telegraph Avenue*, Pulitzer Prize-winning author Michael Chabon delivers another literary masterpiece: a novel of truth and lies, family legends, and existential adventure—and the forces that work to destroy us.

SUMMERLAND
A Novel

From the Pulitzer Prize winning Michael Chabon comes this bestselling novel for readers of all ages that blends fantasy and folklore with that most American coming-of-age ritual: baseball—now in a new edition, with an original introduction by the author.

KINGDOM OF OLIVES AND ASH
Writers Confront the Occupation

A groundbreaking collection of essays by celebrated international writers bears witness to the human cost of fifty years of Israeli occupation of the West Bank and Gaza.

BOOKENDS
A Novel

A brilliant, idiosyncratic collection of introductions and afterwords (plus some liner notes) by *New York Times* bestselling author Michael Chabon—"one of contemporary literature's most gifted prose stylists" (Michiko Kakutani, *New York Times*).